Celebrating

_____

_____

_____

_____

Date _____

Names

_____

_____

_____

Advice and Wishes

_____

_____

_____

_____

_____

_____

_____

_____

_____

_____

_____

_____

Names

Advice and Wishes

Names

_____

_____

_____

Advice and Wishes

_____

_____

_____

_____

_____

_____

_____

_____

_____

_____

_____

_____

Names

Advice and Wishes

Names

_____

_____

_____

Advice and Wishes

_____

_____

_____

_____

_____

_____

_____

_____

_____

_____

_____

Names

Advice and Wishes

_____

_____

_____

_____

_____

_____

_____

_____

_____

_____

_____

_____

_____

_____

Names

_____

_____

_____

Advice and Wishes

_____

_____

_____

_____

_____

_____

_____

_____

_____

_____

_____

Names

Advice and Wishes

Names

_____

_____

_____

Advice and Wishes

_____

_____

_____

_____

_____

_____

_____

_____

_____

_____

_____

Names

Advice and Wishes

Names

_____

_____

_____

Advice and Wishes

_____

_____

_____

_____

_____

_____

_____

_____

_____

_____

_____

Names

_____

_____

_____

Advice and Wishes

_____

_____

_____

_____

_____

_____

_____

_____

_____

_____

_____

Names

_____

_____

_____

Advice and Wishes

_____

_____

_____

_____

_____

_____

_____

_____

_____

_____

_____

_____

Names

_____

_____

_____

Advice and Wishes

_____

_____

_____

_____

_____

_____

_____

_____

_____

_____

_____

Names

Advice and Wishes

Names

Advice and Wishes

Names

Advice and Wishes

_____

_____

_____

Names

Advice and Wishes

Names

_____

_____

_____

Advice and Wishes

_____

_____

_____

_____

_____

_____

_____

_____

_____

_____

_____

_____

Names

_____

_____

_____

Advice and Wishes

_____

_____

_____

_____

_____

_____

_____

_____

_____

_____

_____

_____

Names

_____

_____

_____

Advice and Wishes

_____

_____

_____

_____

_____

_____

_____

_____

_____

_____

_____

_____

Names

_____

_____

_____

Advice and Wishes

_____

_____

_____

_____

_____

_____

_____

_____

_____

_____

_____

Names

_____

_____

_____

Advice and Wishes

_____

_____

_____

_____

_____

_____

_____

_____

_____

_____

_____

Names

_____

_____

_____

Advice and Wishes

_____

_____

_____

_____

_____

_____

_____

_____

_____

_____

_____

Names

_____

_____

_____

Advice and Wishes

_____

_____

_____

_____

_____

_____

_____

_____

_____

_____

_____

_____

Names

_____

_____

_____

Advice and Wishes

_____

_____

_____

_____

_____

_____

_____

_____

_____

_____

_____

Names

_____

_____

_____

Advice and Wishes

_____

_____

_____

_____

_____

_____

_____

_____

_____

_____

_____

Names

Advice and Wishes

Names

Advice and Wishes

Names

Advice and Wishes

Names

_____

_____

_____

Advice and Wishes

_____

_____

_____

_____

_____

_____

_____

_____

_____

_____

_____

Names

_____

_____

_____

Advice and Wishes

_____

_____

_____

_____

_____

_____

_____

_____

_____

_____

_____

Names

_____

_____

_____

Advice and Wishes

_____

_____

_____

_____

_____

_____

_____

_____

_____

_____

_____

_____

Names

Advice and Wishes

Names

_____

_____

_____

Advice and Wishes

_____

_____

_____

_____

_____

_____

_____

_____

_____

_____

_____

Names

_____

_____

_____

Advice and Wishes

_____

_____

_____

_____

_____

_____

_____

_____

_____

_____

_____

Names

Advice and Wishes

Names

_____

_____

_____

Advice and Wishes

_____

_____

_____

_____

_____

_____

_____

_____

_____

_____

_____

Names

Advice and Wishes

_____

_____

_____

_____

_____

_____

_____

_____

_____

_____

_____

_____

Names

Advice and Wishes

Names

_____

_____

_____

Advice and Wishes

_____

_____

_____

_____

_____

_____

_____

_____

_____

_____

_____

Names

Advice and Wishes

Names

_____

_____

_____

Advice and Wishes

_____

_____

_____

_____

_____

_____

_____

_____

_____

_____

_____

Names

Advice and Wishes

Names

Advice and Wishes

_____

_____

_____

Names

_____

_____

_____

Advice and Wishes

_____

_____

_____

_____

_____

_____

_____

_____

_____

_____

_____

Names

Advice and Wishes

Names

_____

_____

_____

Advice and Wishes

_____

_____

_____

_____

_____

_____

_____

_____

_____

_____

_____

Names

Advice and Wishes

_____

_____

_____

_____

_____

_____

_____

_____

_____

_____

_____

_____

_____

Names

Advice and Wishes

Names

_____

_____

_____

Advice and Wishes

_____

_____

_____

_____

_____

_____

_____

_____

_____

_____

_____

Names

_____

_____

_____

Advice and Wishes

_____

_____

_____

_____

_____

_____

_____

_____

_____

_____

_____

_____

Names

_____

_____

_____

Advice and Wishes

_____

_____

_____

_____

_____

_____

_____

_____

_____

_____

_____

Names

_____

_____

_____

Advice and Wishes

_____

_____

_____

_____

_____

_____

_____

_____

_____

_____

_____

Names

_____

_____

_____

Advice and Wishes

_____

_____

_____

_____

_____

_____

_____

_____

_____

_____

_____

Names

Advice and Wishes

Names

_____

_____

_____

Advice and Wishes

_____

_____

_____

_____

_____

_____

_____

_____

_____

_____

_____

Names

Advice and Wishes

Names

Advice and Wishes

Names

_____

_____

_____

Advice and Wishes

_____

_____

_____

_____

_____

_____

_____

_____

_____

_____

_____

_____

Names

_____

_____

_____

Advice and Wishes

_____

_____

_____

_____

_____

_____

_____

_____

_____

_____

_____

_____

Names

Advice and Wishes

_____

_____

_____

_____

_____

_____

_____

_____

_____

_____

_____

_____

_____

_____

Names

_____

_____

_____

Advice and Wishes

_____

_____

_____

_____

_____

_____

_____

_____

_____

_____

_____

_____

Names

Advice and Wishes

Names

Advice and Wishes

Names

Advice and Wishes

Names

_____

_____

_____

Advice and Wishes

_____

_____

_____

_____

_____

_____

_____

_____

_____

_____

_____

Names

Advice and Wishes

Names

_____

_____

_____

Advice and Wishes

_____

_____

_____

_____

_____

_____

_____

_____

_____

_____

_____

Names

_____

_____

_____

Advice and Wishes

_____

_____

_____

_____

_____

_____

_____

_____

_____

_____

_____

Names

_____

_____

_____

Advice and Wishes

_____

_____

_____

_____

_____

_____

_____

_____

_____

_____

_____

_____

Names

_____

_____

_____

Advice and Wishes

_____

_____

_____

_____

_____

_____

_____

_____

_____

_____

_____

Names

_____

_____

_____

Advice and Wishes

_____

_____

_____

_____

_____

_____

_____

_____

_____

_____

_____

_____

_____

Names

_____

_____

_____

Advice and Wishes

_____

_____

_____

_____

_____

_____

_____

_____

_____

_____

_____

Names

Advice and Wishes

_____

_____

_____

_____

_____

_____

_____

_____

_____

_____

_____

_____

_____

_____

Names

Advice and Wishes

Names

Advice and Wishes

Names

_____

_____

_____

Advice and Wishes

_____

_____

_____

_____

_____

_____

_____

_____

_____

_____

_____

_____

Names

_____

_____

_____

Advice and Wishes

_____

_____

_____

_____

_____

_____

_____

_____

_____

_____

_____

_____

Names

Advice and Wishes

Names

Advice and Wishes

_____

_____

_____

_____

_____

_____

_____

_____

_____

_____

_____

_____

_____

Names

_____

_____

_____

Advice and Wishes

_____

_____

_____

_____

_____

_____

_____

_____

_____

_____

_____

Names

Advice and Wishes

_____

_____

_____

_____

_____

_____

_____

_____

_____

_____

_____

_____

_____

_____

_____

Names

Advice and Wishes

_____

_____

_____

_____

_____

_____

_____

_____

_____

_____

_____

_____

_____

_____

Names

Advice and Wishes

Names

Advice and Wishes

Names

_____

_____

_____

Advice and Wishes

_____

_____

_____

_____

_____

_____

_____

_____

_____

_____

_____

Names

Advice and Wishes

Names

_____

_____

_____

Advice and Wishes

_____

_____

_____

_____

_____

_____

_____

_____

_____

_____

_____

_____

Names

_____

_____

_____

Advice and Wishes

_____

_____

_____

_____

_____

_____

_____

_____

_____

_____

_____

Names

_____

_____

_____

Advice and Wishes

_____

_____

_____

_____

_____

_____

_____

_____

_____

_____

_____

_____

Names

_____

_____

_____

Advice and Wishes

_____

_____

_____

_____

_____

_____

_____

_____

_____

_____

_____

_____

Names

_____

_____

_____

Advice and Wishes

_____

_____

_____

_____

_____

_____

_____

_____

_____

_____

_____

Names

_____

_____

_____

Advice and Wishes

_____

_____

_____

_____

_____

_____

_____

_____

_____

_____

_____

Names

Advice and Wishes

Names

_____

_____

_____

Advice and Wishes

_____

_____

_____

_____

_____

_____

_____

_____

_____

_____

_____

_____

Names

_____

_____

_____

Advice and Wishes

_____

_____

_____

_____

_____

_____

_____

_____

_____

_____

_____

Names

Advice and Wishes

Names

_____

_____

_____

Advice and Wishes

_____

_____

_____

_____

_____

_____

_____

_____

_____

_____

_____

_____

Names

Advice and Wishes

Names

_____

_____

_____

Advice and Wishes

_____

_____

_____

_____

_____

_____

_____

_____

_____

_____

_____

Names

Gifts

Names

_____

_____

_____

_____

_____

_____

_____

_____

_____

_____

_____

_____

Gifts

_____

_____

_____

_____

_____

_____

_____

_____

_____

_____

_____

_____

Names   Gifts

_____   _____

_____   _____

_____   _____

_____   _____

_____   _____

_____   _____

_____   _____

_____   _____

_____   _____

_____   _____

_____   _____

_____   _____

_____   _____

Names

_____
_____
_____
_____
_____
_____
_____
_____
_____
_____
_____
_____

Gifts

_____
_____
_____
_____
_____
_____
_____
_____
_____
_____
_____
_____

Names

_____
_____
_____
_____
_____
_____
_____
_____
_____
_____
_____
_____

Gifts

_____
_____
_____
_____
_____
_____
_____
_____
_____
_____
_____
_____

Names

_____

_____

_____

_____

_____

_____

_____

_____

_____

_____

_____

_____

Gifts

_____

_____

_____

_____

_____

_____

_____

_____

_____

_____

_____

_____

Names

_____
_____
_____
_____
_____
_____
_____
_____
_____
_____
_____
_____

Gifts

_____
_____
_____
_____
_____
_____
_____
_____
_____
_____
_____
_____

Names

_____

_____

_____

_____

_____

_____

_____

_____

_____

_____

_____

_____

Gifts

_____

_____

_____

_____

_____

_____

_____

_____

_____

_____

_____

_____

Names

_____
_____
_____
_____
_____
_____
_____
_____
_____
_____
_____
_____

Gifts

_____
_____
_____
_____
_____
_____
_____
_____
_____
_____
_____
_____

Names

_____

_____

_____

_____

_____

_____

_____

_____

_____

_____

_____

_____

Gifts

_____

_____

_____

_____

_____

_____

_____

_____

_____

_____

_____

_____

Names

Gifts

_____

_____

_____

_____

_____

_____

_____

_____

_____

_____

_____

_____

_____

Names	Gifts

Names

Gifts

Names

Gifts

Names

Gifts

_____
_____
_____
_____
_____
_____
_____
_____
_____
_____
_____
_____

Names

_____

_____

_____

_____

_____

_____

_____

_____

_____

_____

_____

Gifts

_____

_____

_____

_____

_____

_____

_____

_____

_____

_____

_____

Names

_____

_____

_____

_____

_____

_____

_____

_____

_____

_____

_____

_____

Gifts

_____

_____

_____

_____

_____

_____

_____

_____

_____

_____

_____

_____

Names

Gifts

_____   _____

_____   _____

_____   _____

_____   _____

_____   _____

_____   _____

_____   _____

_____   _____

_____   _____

_____   _____

_____   _____

_____   _____

Names

Gifts

Names

Gifts

Printed in Great Britain
by Amazon

26061729R00070